PRAISE FOR SOPHIA TERAZAWA'S
WINTER PHOENIX

"Winter Phoenix gathers up the failures of witnessing. When we try to put violence into language, we have recourse only to devious translation, translations of ever-winnowing meanings. In other words, in the face of brutality, words would seem—in Terazawa's speech—to 'stand there and say nothing.' Winter Phoenix constructs, as its central work, the poetic potentials of retribution, using the so-called truths of war, and of war's war-like logics, as its primary material. These poems are indignant, historical intervention. They are themselves the question: 'Who ordered this to happen?'"

—Anaïs Duplan, *Blackspace: On the Poetics of an Afrofuture*

"Terazawa's striking imagery draws attention to the fact that atrocity often unfolds amid beauty and asks us to consider what it means to find stunning images in times of trauma."

—Layla Benitez-James, Harriet Books

Anon

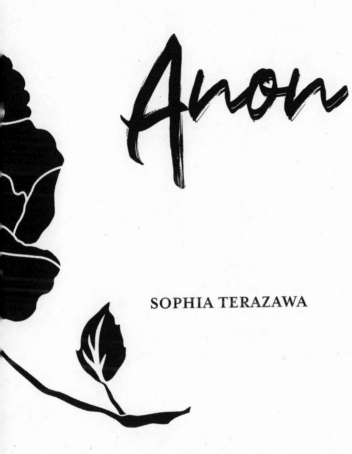

Anon

SOPHIA TERAZAWA

DEEP VELLUM
DALLAS, TX

Deep Vellum Publishing
3000 Commerce St., Dallas, Texas 75226
deepvellum.org · @deepvellum

Deep Vellum is a 501c3 nonprofit literary arts organization
founded in 2013 with the mission to bring
the world into conversation through literature.

Paperback ISBN: 9781646052219
eBook: 9781646052479

Library Of Congress Control Number: 2022945308

Cover art by Irina Kolesnikova
Cover design and typesetting by
David Wojciechowski | www.davidwojo.com

Printed in the United States of America

Contents

STAY

For the muse could not
light another city

with her eyes, you spoke
anon, oil black like mine,

and whoever crossed
that cobbler's

bridge in Ljubljana
would also speak of roots.

So stay, I said. Or kiss
me. No one's

watching, beloved,
but a night

placed
at the far, far end of it.

JULIJA

Prešeren of bronze
facing a window,

not the lake
and ghosts of Tomaž

placed along
his empty hall. One stood

nearby, reading sonnets
in a fortress

dyed to yellow. That
taking shape

was laurel
held above his heart.

Who brought the rose
for Julija? Not you

and certainly not
this poet weeping, Julija.

METELKOVA

Imagine a future at this window, a flurry of gibbons

leaping toward another plane of gold. Or

waiting for translations, anon, you'd signal its flood,

Metelkova spilling over

or hunger also yours, muttering a cobbler's name

and sweetness spilling with music also

crying, Eros! Eros!

You are here in spite of that, these gibbons howling,

Come here. Overgrown with books, our garden of Tivoli.

EROSEROS

Tomaž, who broke a language into three or, as you said
the Latin root for lightning starts with *A*, would also place
adjusting his books, an age of bronze and the mausoleum

blossoming with orchids. He wanted this. I saw you
rearrange his pencils years beyond the wake, and nearby
apes which tumbled underwater formed into this

question of us sounding awfully like midnight. Anon
a gibbon trying outwardly to fly would feign to answer,
yes, this phrasal verb for *A—each week*

a rose

and tiny creatures plucked from earth—anon, the water
taking every word; and still, you flew so close.

ANON

For in that gesture, torn from limb and fruit—

The acrobatic gibbon, Northern Yellow-Cheeked—

An evergreen beginning—

Later, soon, *Anon*, how do I write to you, an adverb?

i.

Anon the arrows fly.

ii.

Cried anon a distant
precipice   our turquoise

dream between

in writing you   anon
the Mekong's tributary grimace

quickly made extinct.

iii.

The crested ape remains mid-air, forced from time.

Deployed in 1965, from Okinawa to Biên Hòa, a combat team precedes
   us,
therefore, timed.

An airborne paw—

iv.

We are difficult. Anon the bells and choir, silt in language
calling, *Eroseros.*

We are slaughtered, past the bells, a precipice of hues.

v.

After Tết, the New Year—

With a leap, you named—

What starts and stops before completion—

Calling genocide, *a serial of dramas,* we, who start or stop
the jagged edge—

A gibbon squats, tearing at a fig.

How shapeless dreams—

Burning delta—

vi.

She who leaps into the water—

vii.

Force of mercury, aluminum,
    the weight of which mistakes a body for its enemy,

skinless streams made sweet—

viii.

In my paws, I hold—

ix.

In your paws   a plume
    swaying easily

the kingfisher nearby.

x.

Here, wounded, crying out, *Eroseros*—

Let me help you—

Stop—

The coiled up—

Recoiled, reddened by its stream; however, in the end—

xi.

Someone wanted mercy.

xii.

Somebody wanted mercy, underwater.

xiii.

Mercy, help us   shimmering and boned
    like empires mistaken, held us for   a people

forced into their rivers.

xiv.

Stop your name—

Sông Hồng   ●   our mother's red begonia

○

○

○

○

○

○

Sông Bến Hải   ●   our DMZ
Sông Hương   ●   perfumed

○

○

○

○

○

○

○

○

○

○   ○

○

Sông Mê Kông   ●   waters singing

Eroseros

Anon the face, as, when a gust hath blown,
Unruffling waters re-collect the shape
Of one that in them sees himself, return'd.

Alfred, Lord Tennyson

Phượng hoàng đua, se sẻ cũng đua.

Anonymous

I

ACROSS THE WILLOW, [SALIX BABYLONICA]

Anon two boats by dusk, rivers peal
    currency of moss.

Bells, vanilla, soft as water. There,
    I touch what's mine.

Fractures speaking, stones forget
    their nature.

i.

Once correcting course, I walk across the bridge.

Returning—   Gibbons branch
    creating sound.

ii.

Younger ones   in ways of written
                lore—

      saying   isn't grief
        splits when diving down.

iii.

Earthen shrapnel—   Were the barracks touched
   by vine, kudzu cities gored?   How do I write
   on genocide, the *after this*, anon?

iv.

   I want to make a prism, less so, white.
   Swirling, gibbons stuff their mouths.

Canto: peaches dry
monumental crimes.

v.

Anon—   The sun reframes a night—   Sleeping
   parts   are walking—   Bells.

Anon the goat is led.
   You make a field around your slaughter.

Vernacular—   Rebirth—   Syncopating
   upside down—

We had a month to speak
   yesterday.

vi.

Anon, removing
to its end—

vii.

Wasn't I   your grief   passing through
an umbra wheel
                        in two
conversations, raised along your ramp?

viii.

    I saw the maple
first of all
                was fir   collecting, therefore

    red
scraped across her knees.

                        Were I
    final, daughter   lyric
passing holds?

    The ship is passing
under.

THE KISS

Walk with me, anon,
arresting thunder.

Should I leave?

The way a siege—
What blossoms underwater?

Should I wave?

For you, breathy rose of peach—
Sink us down, a throne.

It has to be—*Eros*.

That your birthday
led to bombing of a city.

Soon, I shower.

Bus on fire—
Both work out of time, locust.

Yesterday, I walked.

Thorn and nettle disappearing—

THE KISS, AGAIN

Upstairs, the bus on fire held a hem of dress,
peaches after peaches. Soon, the water
infinitely red. I was burnt; surface, charged.

Soft as noun, birds anon parted a glass
announcing limb by limb, going places.

Just, as now, in mouthing, when a mine
hath detonated, bodies recollect as one,
the shape of one who sees in her, returned.

BRAVE AND TINY SCHOLAR

for Brandon and Dot

Calm becomes the trombone, absolutely night; by nights the arrows go.

Hold my foot. For you, I dream a mountain; call me scorpion or scholar.

Suddenly, a year becomes alright. Smaller gods arrive to kiss your paw then your brow. Scorpions arrive; melodies arrive.

Babies pull a book off a shelf. Her name is Yumi; call me Panda.

And I go, forty scars, absolutely dry; war around my ears. Smaller clouds arrive, and I am brave, tiny Panda, scorpion of queens.

WAKE, [ANON]

i.

Nam Phương
final empress bore her lake

oak-white jade
continental. You are older than that.

I turn history gold
dream-fallen ash, therefore, public

amaranth republic
sweet of stem, crepuscular cosmology

wept in dirty paws
wrote of monkeys—

ii.

for you, my flesh
wet silver, amethyst
and rye

myth preceded

then
centuries passed
Nam Phương
without pause, stabbed herself.

A center held.

Gibbons swung
　　　tendrils down, baboon
and ape.

　　　　I rite myself today
detritus knock
　　　divine.

And she who takes the hour
pits a chalice into stone—

iii.

　　　　darker queen of mercy
spare us—

iv.

in 1858, allegedly, *Campagne de Cochinchine*
began, thus our child learned to swim.

Gibbons scratch an anthill.

Yes, the stairwell held us, bones. Gibbon cry.

A father slipped his finger in papaya, therefore,
I was born, queen of chive, milk. Spare us
automatic, bottomless thrones of light.

Lovers bathe inside of me, frayed—

v.

                    imagine us
          a crown

          Palme's death
                         in Sweden

          later, learned
     of Guernica

               imagine that
               lip surpassing massacre.

          Stories of my people
     march into another. How is it love

          something more machine,
     countries lost between us—

LOVE LETTERING, [ANON]

Nigh unto that addressee-formed detritus
   you wrote to me of Cát Tiên parting lowland.

Light caught in between us secondary sounds,
   that habitat upholding language clearing rattan,

fig, that other word for vowel by design.
   Anon, I wrote each gibbon made

extinct, that spark of O—
   that caught between us alloy flint then bush,

attached to that, four paws, attached to that,
   four legs, that upright gibbon staring nigh

unto my heart enclosed upon its outer
   shell becoming land. I wrote to you, anon.

How could you write me back?
   That blast of mine misplacing earth,

that gibbon screeching O—
   that secondary sound catching her secondary

spark, that gibbon without vowel by design
   rewrote our mine, its agate-green extinction.

ROSES, MID-JUNE

No one answered, *Stop*,
that Green Beret
dangling for his photograph
one gibbon by her tail.

I pointed to, anon,
that which might kick
between your books,
that one about a placeless

green turning his boot
into our weaponry of rose.
I could not answer then.
I could not answer now.

Anon, that termed us,
trophy or descendant apishly
remained, withal of rose.

/

Wherefore, I was *O*, that other manual for killing.

Wherefore, paper made our bow from me to you.

/

Or roses through mid-June, that gibbon slept through monsoon.

/

Wherefore striking banyan
into water, we were swept
as when one shoulders to herself
that lance or careful hour,
furled like a country.

Therefore, I was rosy.

/

Leaping like our langur,
        kumquats fell

near bamboo,
        cylinders imploding.

/

Henceforth wired, wax-anointed empress
dawn of rose, sincerely yours, we lettered.

Henceforth stepping manuals for breath
we pressed another mine, becoming *O*—

/

Of underbrush then seedlings
      crystallized our killing, we were altered.

Roses or, anon, in blooming made that mountain
      throne, our gibbons woke up screeching.

/

Tell me how we magistrate.

Altar lies. Our altars never lie.

HOW TO CUT THROUGH WIRE

First: That separating Green and white
        Colonial was stratified. In boarding next
That lowland bulldozed under

Second: You dispensed of *O*—
                That secondary hour
                Circular without though circular within

Our sapper wrote that from her station.

Third: *I am without you.*

/

            Yes, anon—   You wrote—   I, rote of *O*
        that silver-breasted langur

            heavy without cylinder or riverines afloat
another word for force.

/

Anon, that squadron's *O*— that photographic killing
therefore Green Beret had gripped his fist around a tail.

A planted breath, you wrote of other mines and other
sappers lifting up their soles, each step within her altar.

OPERATION END SWEEP

The time had been totally devoted to mine sweeping.
—Navy Task Force 78

What was masked accordingly // that smaller screw behind an eye.

The open *O* unfinished // therefore waiting.

You // its inner chamber pulsing thumb to lip // that was a verb.

Reversing therefore kissed // made crooked into paths.

Anon smooth as green chert // devotional or angelite // a tumbling of
skin.

Of speeding up then breath of formlessness of touch // an uttering of *O*.

That neutralizing air // that sweep of running down.

Breaking screws into a mask // an uttering of steel // for what is cut.

Into a wire or a bomb // we both // that was a noun.

Accordingly // a note from me to you.

PAINTED LANDSCAPE

What remains, anon
crossing your thigh

again that courthouse
wall, a mortar trenched

between us. Amber
light exhaling. Gibbons

hoot then swing.
Cicadas cry a gonging.

I wake mined again
as you pull us in two.

THROWING ROSE, [ANON]

O sprouted tongue, anon, foretold—
    you told me lichen heaped on rock

its belly side, our world of gold in parts.
    I yearned another walk, our skeletal red

morning. Yes, I tripped up wires then
    a rugged thorn standing for time. You threw

after I left, rosy, our kingdom in between.
    In other words, a gibbon intertwining with

her gibbon, asked of us—that neutralizing
    gap between a canister and spark.

In other words, somebody called me monkey,
    once. Somebody called your people monkey,

too, our body less so slurred, our people
    knowing once before that canister and rock

imploding—that
    which therefore clutched a paw clutching

another tail—an ape holding an ape,
    that heart space limbic ache. I held us, burnt

before that time, anon, our golden speech
    against that belly side of love.

I knew to love you then, that gibbon
   in between scratching a tree, its lichen

blooming red and red. She'll make a rose,
   just wait.

TRIPLE BRIDGE

Off course I shook
    rites of us, an imprint
    breath you let me touch;

that triple bridge;
    that genuflecting stone,
    that gibbon thumping tuft,

I told you what was cut
    from Cát Tiên made adverb,
    anon, waiting most joyfully

unarmed;
    that, after ten days, made
    some war our magus O—

I told you then, anon,
    that copal stone
    laid down its triple bridge

of armistice then rose.
    I watched you snap
    each possible upending

rippled by that wire.
    Let us be, I said, an exit
    striding sideways,

Cát Tiên, thus made clean.
    Would you then let me
    O— Would you then

call me kin? Anon,
  what therefore might
  precede us

must be rite of thorn
  accounting for,
  made sweet, that gibbon

thumping at her copal
  face, each copal stone,
  that reservoir unread.

My rite was there,
  I say, in Cát Tiên without age;
  that triple bridge,

our singular collapse,
  that magus *O*— its thread
  standing for green

standing for weight. Anon,
  that circled us.

ANDANTE AT HER LOOM

Blue-seismic near my window, mountains bladed
    platelets hiding underneath. I heard a langur

silvered in her breath, was stolen breathlessly; in counting days,
    unraveled. Yes, I searched.

I was that hoarse and hunchbacked loom.
    Encroaching us, some florets readying for war.

My sister-providential, carefully too pale, that hyacinth and hour
    knocking back. I searched for her.

I searched for you, back then, that poisoned *O*—
    I searched but found her then, anon, bending her paw

to stream, some nation made to swing between each vie.
    How could I write to you that adverb without *O*—

anon, without that apish in-between
    thus clinging to my tail. I was her empress, too.

O, LADY QUEEN OF MERCY

Send me somewhere melding weed with kudzu
bramble, walking sticks for eyes

irradiating outward, helplessly of *O*— kneeling
then shuffling with loom.

O, Lady Queen of Mercy, sing us thicket's
turpentine; that walking through,

unthreading death by chemical defoliant; that langur
draping through her loom our other simile for time;

that loping through some jangling of ink made, once
again, its razing back, who made our simile for blaze.

O, Lady Queen of Mercy, spare her. Spare us fully.

II

BEFORE ROŽNIK HILL WE PASSED A FLUTIST IN THE TUNNEL

Who was what you'd expect of June
apart from the river Ljubljanica and cyclists

panting by or the children of tourists
with their crumbled choco

gelato. I saw one drop her waffle cone and cry
at the bronze fountain where, legend has it,

a poet once sat turning to marble
before her beloved Julija. But

back to the flutist, large inside his
rite of tune and sweeping up, Tivoli which happened

on those waters, too,
we saw

syncopating with each breath, a month
lost between us

and this tempo as we found it, exactly so.

INVASIVE LOVE

To follow winking in this hour of rain
was a Bergman film and reeds

resounding, yes, that was close.

A raven-haired invasive species
written by books in Latin

laid herself across its last translation.

Or when you said the path through bog
became a sword to King Matjaž

buried beneath his mountain.

I answered, and the gibbon's migratory
pattern chanted, *Eroseros*,

wax thickening called to *yes. Or yes,*

when the myth preceded us,
when that gibbon, thrusting out her leg,

answered without language,

when this king of diamonds
carved into alpine stone

finally opened his eyes after five hundred

years, to declare us love, I'd film you
holding my wrists and kiss each one

like a face of lavender.

ALCHEMICAL DEVICES

If my skin pulls out like an atlas : anon   or in Mường La

the portrait of breath deforesting at a rate

which murmurs beyond this chamber's carpeted walls : or bats

which flit about and stare   all over to withstand our rate of dying

I'd see with my mother an old woman hanging up her wash :

in the province   explaining her mother's maiden name was not
  Huynh

but flutes breezing through us   and gone was all that sound

you wanted in 1943 to be so loved and be so loved : alive.

ECHO CHAMBER

After Hera, I said. Not her
grown to a fault and the wild

orchard rewriting autumn
gold—or that which shimmered

aspen in Duluth
we called, a dusk—

what drove us
past her overlook of hours? No,

not earth. Anon
what tumbled down

this waning crescent
flicked on midnight waters

images beyond each precipice
of color;

or what waited
stoking fires made that beast

into its chamber. Comrade,
close to standing,

not her—
knuckles tapping

—*Eroseros.* I was barefoot.

EMPRESS

Nam Phương lifts
her skirt

an onyx braid
unspooled—

Gibbons reaching
hooing air.

She falls tonight
I'm told

into the current.
Roses muddied

moon-floating
tarp. A gibbon

tries again.
Decades bend—

And I'm that
willow.

THIS, OUR EMPRESS AND [ANON]

Leaves tipped into banks of yours, a willow-
mirror   cradling this notebook bound

or as one said
to whish and lash, an installation   you could

walk between us like a sonnet
or then holding out

             the miscellany of us   understood
in careful ways you said   who waited like an empress

holding out her rose and beaded shawl   in spite of us
             and shivering   Nam Phương

who gestured   help us
go   her lover said as jasmines wafted

down a concrete hall   and murmuring
just go   the single hand remained.

SLEEP, [ANON]

i.

As for what shape these windows take
there's truth in that clear morning at Postojna.

Here, I hang a ribbon for your mouth.
Asleep. As for what knights collide a bell

bats fly out; a month, I leave. You left the rose.
Limestone, cocoa, pink, an axolotl poised

below the rest, renewal of our timing. Yes.
You know. As for that longing, windows clear

up truce, our punctuated air. Rain, bitter-balling
up an hour. I'm not sorry. Make that justice.

ii.

Gibbons howl
building up a city
to our last design—

Or, would you melt
the crown, cathedral, ore?

Hai Bà Trưng
on elephants— Here,
I dream of you, knighted.

iii.

Nightly jewels, hold me. Try again.

I taste like silver, candelabra.

iv.

       sleep   my queen
           wherefore a gibbon
   holds up shapeless

          near a window or
our windows   making us
    cavernous

  wish us true

MORNING FREIGHT

True, that buck knife spun a little
farther from its track

surrendering to powerful devices
made available by season. Thus

you spoke of dancing. And the Baltic
Sea you placed in tiny glasses

what you knew of Kosovo
and how our students marched

unarmed, a hyperbolic truth
our maps could make from desert

time or even how
this tongue misplaced aboard

a train could cry despite
its repetition. Or that switch with-

stood our better siege. And holding
to this parcel, what you tore

in 60,000 pieces from your father
winking on then off—so write to me

he begged—would make of him
a mourning. True, that carving

light and scattering of voices
glinted off the blade

and forged a current with its weight.
In spite of that, you wrote to me

then gasped along a skyline
going out and out and out

until even this engine disappeared.
I ran after and saw

your face among the ashen
faces once again

so write to me
I said. Or write to him of cobble-

stone or paint along the walls
that streak of light and cities

red and red and
cattle staring out their slats

and grates of silver
and those Alps

a little farther from the track
before your father

sent out one more letter
every summer.

Would you answer then? Or
would I need to wait?

SAGE POSSESSED THE TWANG

    And every night that banjo clacked against your knees
inertia's careless rhythm, or suppose that

fall by fall, white posies made a simple cloud of doves. Or
where did you so leap to in that civil contradiction? Kids are dying

in your country and my country, too, so tell me:

Comrade, what's the taste of nickel
wound along adjacent terms for revolution? No, I'll go there.

No, I'll go there soon.

Or where in Belgrade, tell me, I may find you? Or in Mỹ Trạch, 1947,
    half of us consumed
became that music's hour. Sing to me, anon

or sing to me without this mouth so filled with feathers.

THUNDERING ROSE

Anon the margin
limitless

shaking out rugs
then light as gourd

you told me
drunk it black.

Averse to rose
thundering

dreams were
crystallized.

*

       —how would I know?

Anon a pot of dirt
  emptied simply a metaphor—was I that foreign?

How would you have known?

*

Symptomatic
    Việt Kiều marching forward—

Sentence incomplete—

*

    At a gallop
    mirrored you
    on benches
    me atop the oak
    and sighing—

*

Leave it be, our rose, you said attached
    an end to delta.

Leave it be
    flying quartz like horses at the margin
dying of our thirst.

III

QUAN ÂM

In this old world
her posture took another
possibility of speech—

or how that upturned
palm meant mercy,
and a red-shanked douc

leapt branch to branch
another line,
each creature after

moving south;
in her longing
Quan Âm murmured,

help us—
reverting this
into another place

of ecocide. I neither
knew her delta
nor that silent heart

which cradled us.

ii.

Gestured Quan Âm:

    Those who'd care for lilies
    bore no children; thus,

I'd bathe her feet
along these shores of Galveston,

a diacritic mark
pronouncing April, "autumn."

Both seemed
like Hanoi, 1955,

my mother tearing at some photo-
graphs. One frightened me

    the most: a garden. Then
one figure inside
        burning.

iii.

From here   soldering
        a language to other branches

smaller gibbons from the northern
        province: one

wrestling with water from a tiny betel leaf
        no bigger than his tiny

charcoal thumb   and turning it over
        found

a set of golden eyes   midrib
        was startled   dropped the leaf.

iv.

Whatever drew those apes from riverbank to   What was writ,

Ink or foliage

In that fodder: a silence I could go on   If our book

Never mind   Was operative for alodine, for instance, compounds of
        a discontinued UC-123

That aircraft maw

In planetary

Misalignment

Or those leaves   In uniform, aghast for air   And gibbons
        merely starting off their sentences but

v.

Quan Âm wept, for every night she lost the perfect memory.

A gibbon sucking at each leaf undid this branching out.

What frightened us became our circular red spark. And near my apish
      heart, I tucked away

your heart. Anon

I'll write to you, therefore, an adverb. Show me where those lines begin,

continue to begin.

In Ljubljana: Church of Saints Cyril and Methodius, a paw would dip

in holy water, thus, become its smaller ape
      and finding you, was startled.

vi.

Queen of Mercy, I said. Help us.

vii.

Urška
dressed in pale goldenrod or bay

dun onstage
welting every coat

bent
fine-tuning her electric
harp; whoever

watched from that corner of history

unable to break in her rising

fingertips

a submergence of horses

particles
which also echoed
Lehrgebäude.

viii.

To discontinue this phrase, each alphabet produced, even so, tiny colonies of apes in my bloodstream.

Someone murmured, Metelkova in summer.

ix.

Warped was
vibrato
which angered us the most

and ghosts of Tomaž
grinning

oracular in kind with tiny

open faces. What also read, "in 1991,"

would also read, "discovery"
or "Republic"

synonymous with a term for "Yugoslav"
wrought in iron,

that yellow
strobe and beneath, Urška

you believed

her talisman of green,

its amaranth of willow

bending
bark or boats

like her country
and my country in one.

x.

Anon
on your wedding day
who brought those silver
bangles? An hour

watched by the docks. Mother
watched

by the flat-screen
TV, and a boatman wept
before his daughter's

funeral. That starkness
suggesting Tomaž

in its marginalia.

On her wedding day, the empress

Nam Phương

who believed in
holding out her ropes
appeased

a demigod who fired with no mercy.

xi.

In a lullaby my mother knew
but long forgot

in a dialect of people
known but long forgotten, she

who'd visit this decade past my death

untended
wild grass or resin

wending stones
blue, so Queen of Mercy, save us. In her

song I
saw that gibbon.

Perched upon a fountain. Pursing
or smacking her funny

gray lips.

A midseason opera

and tourists minding those marble steps of Robba
after rain.

xii.

Past the discotheque   a rose
which fell apart

what you threw in Sarajevo when I left

each season
once more   named in spite of that. Quan Âm

"uninhabited" (*École Français
d'Extrême
Orient, 1967*   or tributaries

starting with a sketch above her eyes)

whatever formed
in correspondence became defacement. I recalled

that twilit

petal's sweetness

near some bone of us, anon.

Silhouettes were painted on wooden benches we ambled by, arm in
arm, leaning into each other as you pointed—gnawing at a strawberry
carton, the coypu flicking her long rubbery tail; or how in that moment, a
shadow tumbled beneath each footbridge becoming metonymy for time,
and a peeved shih tzu, stopping to yap at an art installation downstream,
led to the artist on his second joint—What did you think? He asked at
Metelkova, and I knew he meant the dog; or each month without you
extended like a map repeating its form, and this was Miha fluttering
about his room.

Mala Ljubljanica,
Late Spring.

xiv.

The delta screamed with langurs.

Birds of paradise
emblazoned

summer. Quan Âm
folding up her hands

delivered, "Yes,"

each decade of grief
among those desecrated temples

turning over

even a blistered lip

rushing about its language
mimicking the great blue heron

crying, Eros.

xv.

Firmament of nouns
adorn us.

xvi.

Or perhaps, anon,
I'd hear your father
shearing his roses;

how he left a thorn
in a pile of wires
or flocks of red.

Perhaps I'd call you
when he didn't want
to call you.

Would this be a country
beating back its
language? Say, how in

such brilliance
the poet Tomaž wanted
us to happen.

Say, how copper
thickens, calls to *yes*
or in between

misplaced in time, a carriage
rights that citizen
and gibbons

altering their bones
would rush into us
gasping, light

anon, headlong
into each chamber.

xvii.

Brace for the light. An armistice upon your city
like a fortress in the likeness of bees

thrumming about—or what was peaceful, one murmured

guarding a poem with its life—on catmint
drunk on color and falling,

legs tangled up in each verse or bombs which came

a day early. You were asleep in that park, Tivoli,
pushing a stroller with your knee. In this dream

I was also chased by zombies,

but it was your mother filling up a water vase. You sat
praying at the walls which never opened,

and gardens opened with a shriek. Brace for this—

I remembered and counted every rose. There were two—
one standing for morning, one

for Plečnik drawing up each stone and calling one, a dragon.

xviii.

Anon, I expanded the book to include you in a possibility of paint, like
Monet, splattering linen in careful disorder. When zooming out, head
tilted to one side at an art gallery, you'd become clear about this entire
image. For instance, when replacing your name in this poem, finally
Eros would leave my bed. I set the 4 x 4 centimeter margin to fit a tiny
gibbon sucking her index finger. Would Tomaž write every day? I
forgot to ask you that.

xix.

We could have dreamed of roses.

xx.

Not the red oak
or baby grand west of Denver
turning up one morning

in a cemetery's
maddening cicada swarm

and the grim
wide-faced gibbon
connected to Vietnam

or in that June
wild

mangrove, taken

to catastrophe and its binding
which grows
larger, larger

to include you, anon

in conversation. That was
Brandon, Dot,

Yumi

before you met us

cutting up the pomelo.

xxi.

Red, but not those red hours
Quan Âm pruned with shears,

a sapling
glazed with summer

taking each and every part of us
down to size—

the sequoia, for instance, and its musk,
or one

emperor tamarin
straightening

her tiny mustache and a marmoset
who answered, Yes?—

how could I love them both
as your daughters?

This, anon, was merciful.

xxii.

In that image of a burning ape

Or in a quarry where I was not Vietnamese

But child

Where each hour like a heron making the landing call

Or in citadels, this ecocide as statement

Feigning grace

Or in Quan Âm

Or in our queen of mercy's heart

Or in that burning region which would hunger us for love, anon

Allusively, I told you

In Postojna, nesting in each crevice, brown eyeless bats

To which my mother said in English, Wow

And took one photo on her phone to text Aunt Dao, Aunt Lily,

Uncle Huynh, Aunt Barbara,

My daughter, look, in Europe

And that ape which laughed while shimmering

A mystery of fire

Here my daughter is the poet, queen of mercy, help us.

xxiii.

If the gibbons
scratching at topsoil
were a country
you saw on film
or dreams bound

to paper
which you lifted up
with the trumpet,
queen of mercy, I said,
help us. Or those gibbons

crying out
without a trace of our luminous
temple
were foreign to none.
What she needed, Quan Âm,

neither dialect
nor peering both ways
into a trance
finishing her sentences, I spaced

and memorized your face
dipping over mine.

xxiv.

Each gibbon circumvented its worldly grief,
a silver-backed

incomplete pronouncement

which in death

would also call for Eros. Every being rose

to worship
fluxes of terms astounded by harmonium,

or your friend in Zagreb

who also overdosed on heroin and dragged us both, anon
from this crying coolness of time, or time was just

a lobby of that old Manhattan

erring on speech as well. Staring at the gumbo
was my wonder hitting me for the fourth time. A language formed.

Have mercy, I said.

Or stars were convincing enough.

xxv.

The tiny gibbon which stared
trembling his tiny thumbs,
I won't
hurt you, said I. No one's
gonna hurt you anymore. Anon

this rose
decaying on my doorstep
ending with a cumulus of waiting,

said I was

set in grief at the four corners of your world.
And who could write then

of extinction?

BOOK OF PANDA

For what I found in his mind,
    a place on coconut street

that Panda placed a state
    of emergency, those alarms

which slowed
    a wooing of doves,

I wrote to you. And the book of doves
    which came apart in dialogue.

In your quiet way
    he arrived at this momentum.

And this was Panda
    again flapping his tiny paws

or an air force base
    twenty kilometers away

or the cemetery
    humming with force only

captured on television,
    another sign of each metal cartridge

emptied. Not a word.

IV

SELF-PORTRAIT AS ITO JAKUCHU'S *TWO GIBBONS REACHING FOR THE MOON*

Or this simple reoccurrence
of a scorpion upon its printed scroll

we entered
as in dreaming

        droplets from our wintery
        white borealis

or that shapeless ink
which followed name by poisoned

naming which you turned
and facing yet

        another set of apish eyes
        you wrote to me from Ljubljana

singing softly then
anon I went out drifting

        toward our willow's outer limb
        and working toward another book

was proverb
tripled by design becoming form

a painter-made
translation

how you sat there
with our gibbon wanting more.

AURORA

Torn with brambles, cast into a line
was River Sava.

My present tense arrived misshapen.

Thus, the gorge
too light and babbling. I learned to be

requited also

meant terrain. Three gibbons learning
to jump limb to limb,

a migratory pattern chanting, *Eroseros*

and this afterthought made rose;
or given—

addressee made adverb

split in three directions. Thus, Sava
placed against the mouth of one might

turn into a bramble.

See your hands, beloved,
pressed into

separate constellations.

LESSER BEASTS

At the sanctuary, an orchid tree stood
as if embracing the luminal *Yes*, a paw
reaching for tendrils softened by its name,
the gibbon in her luminous *Now*

echoing a habitat of parallels. I walked,
Anon, into the lovers at their threshold
of ellipses braiding a thought

into their lesser beasts. You translated
a poem, ignored the rest scented with
patchouli. The gibbons lost another
at the sanctuary. One was mouthing, *O*.

ASMR, ROSE, AND GRAPHITE

Or how the mind quiets
easily refastened to what breaks,
a revision of memory—

the market economy—for debate;
and you leaned in,
Anon, to a distant city

made closer in our language
dying out. In all that myrrh,
bold as a thunder's echo

rolling a garden out,
and how you stood there
in your grandfather's sun

meditation, chopping
at the buds.
Medallions: red, pungent,

pewter-gold
refinement. That was how to
love a rosebush, you said.

Comrade, beneath
the lead of your heart
in my memory—to whisper

that, Anon—forgive me, promise
none of what eroded
in our book

covered the stones in Tivoli.

APPETITE

In the book, I rewrote a banyan tree as an image of ghosts
groaning from the earth; of green tenderizing the vowels—
O, especially; of gibbons thrown to the wind and steel twisting
along the sides of a mill. I knew it then as a dream, my back
turned to you. And the snakes felt as if they could be one.

TRANSLATING AN HOUR AT THE LOOM

Or this paper made of dust and borders
torn from hours spent away from you, Anon.

To call this map displacement or my pulse
as they had labeled us, *subhuman*, I was sure

that tiny gibbon crouched beyond her
sanctuary. There, my empress, Quan Âm,

held out both her ashen palms, renounced
a throne and troubadours upon this edge.

To dust back from her hour, faces peering
down a crystalline black water. You were

there, sensing its other mouth, a parchment
moon's reflection as we murmured, *Eroseros*.

ON THE NATURE OF MYRRH

Or the secret of lips pressing an arc
to the mouth. I could hold

entire nights in that, Anon, address you
by your name, and pique

the entire mountain with that, too; so
you were told. An ape flew

from her tree. I made a minute by digging
into this, climbing a banister;

Anon, there was Tomaž who held open
his hall to publishers and elm

leaves, all alike, after a nightmare. Anon,
I said to you, faltering

the ghost who flounced past the yellowing
of trees; those trees you

later blessed. A gibbon picked her toes
and stared out past the delta.

Or the nature of a book, neither
written in your language or

my feet drumming Metelkova; the myrrh-
smoked hall again and Tomaž

in his corner, on a wooden crate; the men
smoking nearby; the night

truly in prayer; and I whispered, Anon,
just stay right here beside me.

COFFEE PORTRAIT OF A DANDELION CHILD

On my paper, the florets stood and reappeared
after February. Quan Âm, my empress,
or the ceremony of Horus glowed in the night.

You wrote to me, Anon, that the passage
underwater at Postojna, like a subterranean
axolotl, stood in the face of its extinction.

I could glean from this, your message
surfacing our countries unknown where
we'd meet. Two dandelions from coffee

quickly disappearing into a constellation,
and the quiet axolotl sniffing at these peach-
pink roses blossoming inside your garden.

BARREL SONG

At the center of a photograph: the couple
pressing their thighs toward each other,
notes of home, a conical shape roving

waywardly; and you were there, Anon,
the second made invisible among glass
and shutters. The gibbon in a tree made

for herself, a shadow. Play me that song,
Anon, a castanet of apes, something about
the horizon and a princess waiting there.

PYGATHRIX NEMAEUS

Looking back, I should have known
then pulling out her face

that red-shanked douc, millennia's desire
casting rivers in no river.

You were trodden without wires. Noted—
Threatened—by one species

ordered to its brink. I told you then, Anon,
our rose brought up to drink

made pale beneath our surface-facing stream.
That douc pushing her mouth

over each fig, a metaphor for green.
Nobody knew. Nobody should have known.

You called me back, Anon. And I was
through that pillar of our country

ordered to its brink. That langur's golden
throne—*Extinct*—and I was gone.

GIBBONS HOWLING

Later on
that scorpion
I enter you

anon, a faded
tree.

A shapeless
life—

Our name
I called you
then. Could

you thus
write to me?

My dear *Anon*

our trees
that pentacle
of shift

that wording
for its word

another word
for life—

proverbial
anon, to wait

for one
who has in us
returned.

ACKNOWLEDGMENTS

amberflora: "Throwing Rose, [Anon]"

ANMLY: "Brave and Tiny Scholar," "The Kiss," "The Kiss, Again," "Across the Willow [Salix Babylonica]"

Berkeley Poetry Review: "Anon," "Thundering Rose," "Lesser Beasts," "ASMR, Rose, and Graphite," "Appetite"

Cordite Poetry Review: "Wake, [Anon]"

Oxidant|Engine: "Love Lettering, [Anon]," "Roses, Mid-June," "How to Cut through Wire," "Operation End Sweep," "Painted Landscape," "Triple Bridge," "Andante at Her Loom," "O, Lady Queen of Mercy"

Sepia Journal: "Self-Portrait as Ito Jakuchu's *Two Gibbons Reaching for the Moon*," "This, Our Empress and [Anon]," "Morning Freight"

Sixth Finch: "Book of Panda"

Brief sections of "Anon" were modified for DVAN, appearing in a collective exhibit and chapbook, *She Who Has No Master(s): Would That*, and selected to be reprinted in *hush: a journal of noise*.

"Morning Freight" was featured in episode #698 of *The Slowdown*, hosted by Ada Limón.

Photo by Callisto Moses

Sophia Terazawa is a performance artist and poet. She is the author of two chapbooks, *I AM NOT A WAR* (Essay Press), a winner of the 2015 Essay Press Digital Chapbook Contest, and *Correspondent Medley* (Factory Hollow Press), winner of the 2018 Tomaž Šalamun Prize. Her debut collection, *Winter Phoenix* (Deep Vellum, 2021), was named a 2021 finalist for the Big Other Award in Poetry and CLMP'S Firecracker Award in Poetry. She currently teaches in the MFA program at Virginia Tech.

Thank you all
for your support.
We do this for you,
and could not do
it without you.

DEEP
VELLUM

PARTNERS

pixel ||| texel

EMBREY FAMILY
FOUNDATION

ALLRED
CAPITAL MANAGEMENT
of
RAYMOND JAMES®

ADDITIONAL DONORS, CONT'D

Mark Haber
Mary Cline
Maynard Thomson
Michael Reklis
Mike Soto
Mokhtar Ramadan
Nikki & Dennis Gibson
Patrick Kukucka
Patrick Kutcher
Rev. Elizabeth & Neil Moseley
Richard Meyer

Scott & Katy Nimmons
Sherry Perry
Sydneyann Binion
Stephen Harding
Stephen Williamson
Susan Carp
Susan Ernst
Theater Jones
Tim Perttula
Tony Thomson

SUBSCRIBERS

Alan Glazer
Amber Williams
Angela Schlegel
Austin Dearborn
Carole Hailey
Caroline West
Courtney Sheedy
Damon Copeland
Dauphin Ewart
Donald Morrison
Elizabeth Simpson
Emily Beck
Erin Kubatzky
Hannah Good
Heath Dollar

Heustis Whiteside
Hillary Richards
Jane Gerhard
Jarratt Willis
Jennifer Owen
Jessica Sirs
John Andrew Margrave
John Mitchell
John Tenny
Joseph Rebella
Josh Rubenoff
Katarzyna Bartoszynska
Kenneth McClain
Kyle Trimmer
Matt Ammon

Matt Bucher
Matthew LaBarbera
Melanie Nicholls
Michael Binkley
Michael Lighty
Nancy Allen
Nancy Keaton
Nicole Yurcaba
Petra Hendrickson
Ryan Todd
Samuel Herrera
Scott Chiddister
Sian Valvis
Sonam Vashi
Tania Rodriguez

AVAILABLE NOW FROM DEEP VELLUM

SHANE ANDERSON • *After the Oracle* • USA

MICHÈLE AUDIN • *One Hundred Twenty-One Days* • translated by Christiana Hills • FRANCE

BAE SUAH • *Recitation* • translated by Deborah Smith • SOUTH KOREA

MARIO BELLATIN • *Mrs. Murakami's Garden* • translated by Heather Cleary • *Beauty Salon* • translated by Shook • MEXICO

EDUARDO BERTI • *The Imagined Land* • translated by Charlotte Coombe • ARGENTINA

CARMEN BOULLOSA • *Texas: The Great Theft* • translated by Samantha Schnee • *Before* • translated by Peter Bush • *Heavens on Earth* • translated by Shelby Vincent • MEXICO

CAYLIN CAPRA-THOMAS • *Iguana Iguana* • USA

MAGDA CÂRNECI • *FEM* • translated by Sean Cotter • ROMANIA

LEILA S. CHUDORI • *Home* • translated by John H. McGlynn • INDONESIA

MATHILDE WALTER CLARK • *Lone Star* • translated by Martin Aitken & K. E. Semmel • DENMARK

SARAH CLEAVE, ed. • *Banthology: Stories from Banned Nations* •
IRAN, IRAQ, LIBYA, SOMALIA, SUDAN, SYRIA & YEMEN

TIM COURSEY • *Driving Lessons* • USA

LOGEN CURE • *Welcome to Midland: Poems* • USA

ANANDA DEVI • *Eve Out of Her Ruins* • translated by Jeffrey Zuckerman • *When the Night Agrees to Speak to Me* • translated by Kazim Ali MAURITIUS

DHUMKETU • *The Shehnai Virtuoso* • translated by Jenny Bhatt • INDIA

PETER DIMOCK • *Daybook from Sheep Meadow* • USA

CLAUDIA ULLOA DONOSO • *Little Bird*, translated by Lily Meyer • PERU/NORWAY

LEYLÂ ERBIL • *A Strange Woman* •
translated by Nermin Menemencioğlu & Amy Marie Spangler • TURKEY

RADNA FABIAS • *Habitus* • translated by David Colmer • CURAÇAO/NETHERLANDS

ROSS FARRAR • *Ross Sings Cheree & the Animated Dark: Poems* • USA

ALISA GANIEVA • *Bride and Groom* • *The Mountain and the Wall* •
translated by Carol Apollonio • RUSSIA

FERNANDA GARCÍA LAO • *Out of the Cage* • translated by Will Vanderhyden • ARGENTINA

ANNE GARRÉTA • *Sphinx* • *Not One Day* • *In Concrete* • translated by Emma Ramadan • FRANCE

NIVEN GOVINDEN • *Diary of a Film* • GREAT BRITAIN

JÓN GNARR • *The Indian* • *The Pirate* • *The Outlaw* • translated by Lytton Smith • ICELAND

GOETHE • *The Golden Goblet: Selected Poems* • *Faust, Part One* •
translated by Zsuzsanna Ozsváth and Frederick Turner • GERMANY

SARA GOUDARZI • *The Almond in the Apricot* • USA

NOEMI JAFFE • *What Are the Blind Men Dreaming?* •
translated by Julia Sanches & Ellen Elias-Bursac • BRAZIL

CLAUDIA SALAZAR JIMÉNEZ • *Blood of the Dawn* • translated by Elizabeth Bryer • PERU

PERGENTINO JOSÉ • *Red Ants* • MEXICO

TAISIA KITAISKAIA • *The Nightgown & Other Poems* • USA

SONG LIN • *The Gleaner Song: Selected Poems* • translated by Dong Li • CHINA

GYULA JENEI • *Always Different* • translated by Diana Senechal • HUNGARY

DIA JUBAILI • *No Windmills in Basra* • translated by Chip Rossetti • IRAQ

JUNG YOUNG MOON • *Seven Samurai Swept Away in a River* • *Vaseline Buddha* •
translated by Yewon Jung • SOUTH KOREA

ELENI KEFALA • *Time Stitches* • translated by Peter Constantine • CYPRUS

UZMA ASLAM KHAN • *The Miraculous True History of Nomi Ali* • PAKISTAN

KIM YIDEUM • *Blood Sisters* • translated by Jiyoon Lee • SOUTH KOREA

JOSEFINE KLOUGART • *Of Darkness* • translated by Martin Aitken • DENMARK

ANDREY KURKOV • *Grey Bees* • translated by Boris Dralyuk • UKRAINE

YANICK LAHENS • *Moonbath* • translated by Emily Gogolak • HAITI

JORGE ENRIQUE LAGE • *Freeway: La Movie* • translated by Lourdes Molina • CUBA

FOUAD LAROUI • *The Curious Case of Dassoukine's Trousers* •
translated by Emma Ramadan • MOROCCO

FORTHCOMING FROM DEEP VELLUM

CHARLES ALCORN • *Beneath the Sands of Monahans* • USA

MARIO BELLATIN • *Etchapare* • translated by Shook • MEXICO

CARMEN BOULLOSA • *The Book of Eve* • translated by Samantha Schnee • MEXICO

CHRISTINE BYL • *Lookout* • USA

MIRCEA CĂRTĂRESCU • *Solenoid* • translated by Sean Cotter • ROMANIA

TIM CLOWARD • *The City that Killed the President* • USA

JULIA CIMAFIEJEVA • *Motherfield* • translated by Valzhyna Mort &
Hanif Abdurraqib • BELARUS

PETER CONSTANTINE • *The Purchased Bride* • USA

FREDERIKA AMALIA FINKELSTEIN • *Forgetting* •
translated by Isabel Cout & Christopher Elson • FRANCE

EMILIAN GALAICU-PĂUN • *Canting Arms* •
translated by Adam J. Sorkin, Diana Manole, & Stefania Hirtopanu • MOLDOVA

ALISA GANIEVA • *Offended Sensibilities* • translated by Carol Apollonio • RUSSIA

ALLA GORBUNOVA • *It's the End of the World, My Love* •
translated by Elina Alter • RUSSIA

GISELA HEFFES • *Ischia* • translated by Grady C. Ray • ARGENTINA

TOSHIKO HIRATA • *Is It Poetry?* •
translated by Eric E. Hyett & Spencer Thurlow • JAPAN

KB • *Freedom House* • USA

YANICK LAHENS • *Sweet Undoings* • translated by Kaiama Glover • HAITI

ERNEST MCMILLAN • *Standing: One Man's Odyssey through the Turbulent Sixties* • USA

FISTON MWANZA MUJILA • *The Villain's Dance* • translated by Roland Glasser •
DEMOCRATIC REPUBLIC OF CONGO

LUDMILLA PETRUSHEVSKAYA • *Kidnapped: A Story in Crimes* •
translated by Marian Schwartz • RUSSIA

SERGIO PITOL • *Taming the Divine Heron* • translated by George Henson • MEXICO

N. PRABHAKARAN • *Diary of a Malayali Madman* •
translated by Jayasree Kalathil • INDIA

THOMAS ROSS • *Miss Abracadabra* • USA

JANE SAGINAW • *Because the World Is Round* • USA

SHUMONA SINHA • *Down with the Poor!* • translated by Teresa Fagan • INDIA/FRANCE

KIM SOUSA, MALCOLM FRIEND, & ALAN CHAZARO, eds. • *Até Mas: Until More—An
Anthology of LatinX Futurisms* • USA

MARIANA SPADA • *The Law of Conservation* • translated by Robin Myers • ARGENTINA

SOPHIA TERAZAWA • *Anon* • USA

KRISTÍN SVAVA TÓMASDÓTTIR • *Herostories* •
translated by K. B. Thors • ICELAND

YANA VAGNER • *To the Lake* •
translated by Maria Wiltshire • RUSSIA

SYLVIA AGUILAR ZÉLENY • *Trash* •
translated by JD Pluecker • MEXICO

LIU ZONGYUAN • *The Poetic Garden of Liu Zongyuan* •
translated by Nathaniel Dolton-Thornton & Yu Yuanyuan • CHINA